Platonic Love

Platonic Love

Poems by
Michael J. Bugeja

Orchises Washington 1991

To Lyn

Copyright © 1991 Michael J. Bugeja

Library of Congress Cataloging-in-Publication Data
Bugeja, Michael
    Platonic love: poems by Michael Bugeja
    p. cm.
    ISBN 0-914961-21-6 : $10.00
    I. Title
PS3552.U387P4 1991
811'54—dc20
                                                      90-19734
                                                            CIP

ACKNOWLEDGEMENTS

Certain of these poems originally appeared in the following journals:
Alaska Quarterly Review, Amelia, Antioch Review,
Atavist, AWP Newsletter, Blue Unicorn, Cape Rock,
Chariton Review, Cross Timbers Review, The Georgia Review,
Hawai'i Review, Hollins Critic, The Kenyon Review,
Manhattan Poetry Review, Nebraska Review,
New England Review & Bread Loaf Quarterly, Newport Review,
Poet & Critic, Poet Lore, Southern Poetry Review,
and *West Branch.*

The poem "Dolphins" was reprinted in *Anthology of*
Magazine Verse & Yearbook of American Poetry, 1989 edition.

This book was completed with the assistance
of a grant from the National Endowment for the Arts,
a federal agency.

Cover: Diane Sears-Bugeja
Composition: Christina Nuckols & Dick Bean,
E.W. Scripps School, Ohio University,
Athens, Ohio

Manufactured in the U.S.A.

Published by Orchises Press
P.O. Box 20602 Alexandria, VA 22320-1602

G 6 E 4 C 2 A

Contents

Part One

The Keepers   3
Thaw   4
When I Feel Your Soul,
    I Reach For You With These Arms   6
Systems   7
Oracle of Oklahoma   9
Patient   10
Material Goods   11
Tender   12
Geographies   14
Love, Hate: The Life We Learn   16
Fear, Fate: What Love Has To Lose   18

Part Two

The Converts   21
The Art of Amnesia   22
South   23
Man In The Kitchen   24
Asylum, At Least On Paper   26
What The Waitress Sees   27
Liebe Und Literatur   29
The Brevity And Permanence of Snow   30
Self-Portrait   31
Dolphins   32
Angelic Love   33

Part Three

Discovery 37

The Unnatural Act Of Our Making 38

The Half-Life Of Love 39

Carpe Diem 40

Realism 41

Poets in Love 42

The Clock 43

Sonata And Fugue, A Love Poem 44

Stormy 45

Stay 47

Anthem: Love And The Antipodes 49

I Know 50

Moon, Love: Whereof I Swear
Never Again To Write 51

Salzburg 52

Part Four

Heresy 57

The Bittersweet Days 58

The Night That Should Have Been Ours 59

Harmony 60

Art By Association 61

Silence 62

The Restoration 63

Sudden Love 64

Forgiveness 66

Navigating The Asteroid Belt,
Zero Visibility 68

Blackout, Again, In New York 69

How To End A Romance 70

Platonic Love

I.

When we kiss the lips are closed,
The hips politely apart. We have lain
Open-mouthed with strangers, hip to hip.

II.

When we touch, we are laced to the boot,
Caress cloth. Piece by piece
Others unribbon us, shape our clay.

III.

When we're alone we polarize,
North to north. We use our lips
For talk, our hips to walk away.

IV.

No one wants our bodies
As much as we do.

Part One

The Keepers

A.D. 1329

We made a pact. Close your eyes
And remember it in the cloud-studded
Blue of your soul. You can see us
As we were then, the coarse
Homespun wool of your smock,
The pantaloons and sash. The coarser
Cut of my one good garment in strips

Like the pulled-apart gauze
Of a martyr. I would do it
Again, I would suffer the merciless,
Ring-bearing thumb of the manor-lord
Who found us outside Lyon, site
Of the great fair: the conical tent
And colorful, triangular banner

A lineage in the woods. Of course
We had to die. You belonged to another
And were thankful for the week
Fate had given us, the morning
Without work and the twilight
Without pain. You did not flinch
When they tore the cloth from your body

Like a sculpture. I had to watch
You go before me. Even the vassal
With his innate ken of genetics
Could not unravel the pact.
We sealed it where no one would
Look: between the fifth and sixth
Chromosomes of the heart.

Thaw

I had better begin with the horse
Nobody wanted to break
Long ago. You did, and you speak of him
Lovingly as you might speak of me
In that Northern nasal twang

I obey like an animal. Alone,
Atop the massive swayback of Appaloosa,
You barrel on a butte of snow
That spews in late spring like slush
In my city. But this is Dakota

And you are a girl, so thoroughly one
You circle and stop, dismount to inspect
A purple patch of flower
That glistens in the white. To this day
Purple is your favorite color

And what happens next, the only rule
You enforce. Naturally, you pluck it.
The horse beside you is beautiful
As a hyacinth is beautiful in the snow,
And you are a friend to beauty, even then

Obsessed with it as snow is with white,
A color that kills on the tundra.
And it wilts, the flower
That may have been thankful
For the warmth of your palm,

Willing to leave the limbo
Of weather. You don't see it
This way. Beauty, you say, is a moment.
I give you plenty of those
But no flowers, though I want to

Blossom too early in a season
That only feels like spring
And is barren, deadly, white.
I should end now with the horse
Whose only role in this was to run.

When I Feel Your Soul,
I Reach for You with These Arms

I know now what you mean by fate,
The love that makes its own commitment,
However clumsy, and overcomes a woman
Whose only vow was to free herself of men,
To use their bodies as they have used hers,
For the hell of it. Love takes that woman
And gives her to a man who feels her soul,

But wants the body too. He doesn't want it
Selfishly, for ego, or any cocksure
Reason that she can reject like a lover
Who wears out the night. No, he is after
Cliches—body and soul—that beauty
She never dreamed could be
Within reach. It is not that simple.

Nobody understands. This man
Comes to her when she is high
On friends, a little melody and smoke
To forget before bed. She has to
Answer the door and dismiss him,
Her only joy: he arrives like clockwork
Not out of jealousy—another cliche—

But because he has felt her soul.
This is not beauty. This is hell
Love invents for those who risk
Anything in its name. So they step
Closer to that light and cannot stop
Or will lose each other. *We know that.*
We resign ourselves. It is our lot.

Systems

A thousand Ph.D.'s applauded me
Last night. They didn't want to clap. They do not
Do it well. And there I stood, rather
Shakily, on a patch of masking tape
Indelibly marked "Award Winner One,"

Knowing what was up: how some, the scientists,
Say, were observing me like a specimen
For a shiver or bead of sweat, anything
Biological to betray the public
Self. Or the artists, mindful of image,

Framing me for ego, but wanting the plaque.
Or the tenured, the emeriti. How like magi
They divine an age: thirty, or thereabouts,
Way too young for this, way too young!
And a woman I love, even younger, watching me

But wary about my nerves, whether I would drop
Like a pledge who is hazed by the house, pinned by it.
I did not drop. I sweated it out, ego-less
And embarrassed, and yes, too young. But she,
Whom I want more than honor or fame, had to leave

Raving about the system of which I am
A part, raving about the bull and banter,
Fed up with it, as I am with the institution
Of love. The day before, this woman came to me
To defend another master of banter and bull,

The jazzier sort, a guy with whom I have longed
To trade places, only because she sees
The system of me and honors it like a contract
Between us. She keeps none with him, believes
"He likes me for myself." She was ready

To go on, a speech she had planned for me
And blocked, mid-sentence, as if something had
Startled her. She began to study me
Helpless in my office, framed by degree,
Ego, age, and biology at work. She saw more

Than mere desire, easy to spot in a man,
And I saw more than she had given anybody
Credit for: I liked her for the Self,
An entity we knew, because we were
In danger of losing it. Something clicked

Finally in both of us, a spark of fate
That singes the brain: nobody else matters.
We are in this together, on stage, in public
With no system to guide us but love.
Bonafide. Unadulterated. *Real.*

Oracle of Oklahoma

If I could pilgrim such a place
I would not ask the muse
Who lords below the clay

To make the milo meet a yield,
The ewe to mutton up and fleece
The feeder lot of cash,

Or corn to silo miser-like.
Nor would I flock a church,
Fundamental in these parts

As a purse, or divine
Geologically, devout as a driller.
Rights in this matter are neither

Mineral or realistic. I'd ask
For faith, not—my God—
In afterlife but love,

Which you fulfill like prophecy
In the least likely of places:
Oklahoma, where we can lose ourselves

Looking for answers.

Patient

My love, the woman I leave for a man
She will sleep with, clomping up the stairs
Like clockwork, no time for anything
But a word: patient. She says it,
And the next thing I know I am out
On the street, out, like that, a wink.
I see them in the window, silhouettes.

What happened here?

Thirty-three, I suffer the cliches
Of success: jealousy, loneliness, desire.
Whiskey helps. You swallow, the fire
Flares a little, and goes out. You land
Where you can't remember getting to,
Like a ditch, the car idling,
A siren that slaps you awake:

Patient.

She will sketch a picture of me
As cameo, a man who says too much,
Quiet on canvas, and I will write
About a word whose root is time,
Whose light is unseen but on its way,
A star so new it means to shine
If we can just wait long enough.

Material Goods

> *It was a little like a middle-age man falling in love again. A remarkable thing to witness, and embarrassing, too.*—Raymond Carver

Let me explain before you chalk it up
To sex, or worse, the need for it. Yes,
I'm on a binge—jewelry, watch, coat,
Breakfast in the bed we lay upon once,
Clothed to the shoes but together,
Beauty and beast—"frog," a pet name.
These days I feel like a frog, green

And jumpy. Something's stirring inside
That has to do with the heart,
A kind of beating. It happened that way
With my father. Growing up, I took
A bruise for love, and when love came
Before he died, it came with a binge:
Material goods, heirlooms to boots.

Honey, I love that pendant you wear
With my words—*with you always.*
Fact is, I fear how long we'll "be."
The body, I know, is going. The heart,
I know, is not. That doesn't explain
The gifts you wear or wrap around you.
Maybe it does.

Tender

You come from the bar and flop
Beside me on the bed, my palm
Pulling you to the grove of my chest,
A dissolve. The last drink
You pour like a tip for yourself

Before closing, one-handed driver
Who sips at the light and blinks
Her way home. I can have it,
You whisper, and I am unsure
What you mean: life, love,

Or the lemony cup at the headboard.
This is a time I can savor,
One for the road. Already
The blouse is unbuttoned,
The body in a deep-heave

Of sleep. I can have you
Here, the small breasts
Flat on my belly, or here—
The lithe legs astraddle
And limp. I do not know

How the parts on this night
Become one and lose meaning
Like parts of a cocktail
You swirl to change color, the breast
No longer a thing to be sipped,

No longer a lip or a leg. I explain
Only now, months and the lovers
Parading between us. You are
Thinking again about touch
But confuse it with desire:

When I talk about need—
The body that is a bed,
The palm that is a pillow—
I am looking for a way
Love has to heal. The way home.

Geographies

In all your fantasies, nights on the farm your father lost
In the formative years, livestock and livelihood
Property now of Liberty Savings, next to the Otasco
You would live behind on Main Street—yes, Main Street
Of a dustbowl town—never did you suspect a poem,

Or want it. What you wanted, I had: learning, a way out
Of loneliness and landscape, of the impossible
Expanse. What I wanted, you had: beauty, a way in
To a world of flesh and possibility, of conceivable
Positions. This is how it plays in the Panhandle,

The barter of body for mind. Imagine such trade,
Believe in it as the Baptists do the apple,
Tree of Knowledge. I had an orchard-full,
Free for the picking. But this was the fallen Eden
Of unirrigated Oklahoma, where condemnation is common

As American pie, and you—a Susan or Debbie, lovelier
Than sin in all its genres—came today to deal.
We looked at each other, so much produce, and named
The price: lines, a library of them, for love
At the Holiday Inn, compliments County Extension.

★

Books, books. Where would I be without them? Some factory
Probably in Newark or Patterson, a cancer blooming by now
In the kidneys, a wife who bingos at Sacred Heart.
I could leave any time. I could look across the swamp
And see New York, the Big Apple, and dream the somebody

I'd never be. This is my geography, or was. I traded
A skyline for sky, and made my mark. So I teach
In towns with names like Alex and Bradley, Mustang,
Where women as beautiful as you are wed before
They dream of escape, if allowed to dream at all:

*You have the key. You have driven your husband's pickup
To a hotel where everyone knows you, the clerk at the desk,
The roughnecks at the bar, and parked outside Room 24B.
You will knock, politely at first, and open the door
To an empty room. You will find a poem where payment was due:*

The bed. I am making you do this. I am making you think
Geographies, spacial and physical. Already I am home,
Knowing you will hate me but keep the books,
Which I would have given you anyway. Christ,
There must be hundreds like you. Worse, like me.

Love, Hate: The Life We Learn

We come here to be alone, to complain
As lovers complain with a little longing,
Silvery words that rise and spark
The mist of a Panhandle night. The city
Put new benches in, so we try one out
And pretend the low-rent panorama
Shadowed and sheltered by maple
Is an enclave abroad where we wintered.

It could be worse, you say, when I doubt
Love and work: lighten up. I could lose myself
In the gathering fog, a half-fog that cuts
The silhouettes of an oncoming someone
And his dog. The haze hovers enough
To hide us. But the animal senses us there,
And the person approaches: a boy
In middle school maybe, the chew he spits

A giveaway. You ask the dog's name, Max,
And I think how important that is,
Name of the Doberman nuzzling your hand.
The boy, whose name we do not want
To become too familiar, hunkers
In the mud. He brags in a marbly drawl
The dog is new and trained for the pit.
Max, meanwhile, has slithered to sleep.

Doberman'll attack anybody. Cops, mailmen—
The sputum flies from the crook of his mouth—
Anybody. What about teachers? I ask,
Lightening up. *If you want to kill a teacher,*
He says, serious as one, *get yourself a suit*
With patches like they wear, and stuff it
Best you can for the bite. Then you beat that dog,
You cuss it. He spits again. *It'll work.*

He is getting friendly now, familiar.
He is in a park with his own kind,
Folk who want to kill. *Got me a pit bull*
Home hates blacks, and a nigger-boy
I know wasn't scared none by that bark.
So I said he might learn the easy way
By listening or the hard way—spit,
I can almost predict it now—*by running.*

We hear enough. We talk to each other
As if the boy who has figured us out
Left long ago. We ignore him like teachers
Sometimes do, and he becomes another object
In the mud. A stump, a block of wood.
We link arms and leave, suddenly unsettled
Again. A silence descends as it does here
Before a thunderclap, and you stop. You feel

A little sadness for the boy. Maybe we should
Go back and keep company with him awhile,
You say, the goodness I usually admire
Welling up like an aura in the haze
And healing him somehow. I want to
Believe that. But I am in love tonight
With my own problems, darker than the hate
Some of us learn the hard way, living this life.

Fear, Fate: *What Love Has To Lose*

The brain nearly went, the breakdown
Where the poem lies, or believes
It lies, in the right cortex, and I wanted
You more than ever. Time was running

My life—overrunning yours—lording over it
Like prey. *How could you know?*
A sleuth, you pieced the parts as a writer
Puts a scheme to rhyme: first, the slant

Our talks undertook with body and soul,
The reading between lines, the fine print
Of telepathy wee hours and weekends,
The revision of wills, the clash of them

Before epiphany: one of us was dying
And being tight-lipped about it.
You didn't weep as a woman would
In love lyrics. You told me where to go,

A hell that hospitals know, and waited
As I had to wait, looking dead-middle
At that hourglass, that metaphor we mix
At any moment and call second chance.

Part Two

The Converts

              1119 A.D.

I see her alone in the confessional
And beg her hand, which she bestows
Easily as penance. I never know
When she will come to me. I open
The slat and hear the others,
The familiar transgressions: greed
In a good year, lust in a bad.

It is a bad year. A priest can only
Cross himself and hope the heart
In its own black chamber rises up
When she is there, vowing
Love like candlelight will flare
Soon as Venus conjoins with Mars.
I cannot wait much longer

Hidden in the heath, watching
The finespun silk of her gown float
Ghostlike on the grass: silvery.
The abbey is asleep before matins,
A heavenly hour. This may be the sky
We have prayed for, night after night,
Lyric as obsession. I recite her

Name like a psalm, trilling it
In Saxon. Things begin to happen:
The high-cone hat with a slip-knot of lace
Sails off her head and silhouettes
Across the moon. *I will remember it
A millennium later!* She beckons me
To join her as the brethren become

Songbirds on the last day of a life.

The Art of Amnesia

Maybe if I write this out, give it up
To gears of meter, caesura, and rhyme,
I will not clang inside like a cup

Stung by a spoon, cracked by it. I am
That breakable. Say I time this self-
Consuming prophecy just right with iamb

And measure, lyric and line on a shelf
Beside amphibrachs in a cupboard.
Would canon or craft in any way quell

The desire tonight to hold her, hoard
Lover-like the anapest of her heart?
I don't know. So imagine my working toward

Conclusion, the easy denouement, the sort
A reader with a yen for Jung would prove
My kind of broken dish. It is a start,

However dim, for when the triplets move
Leisurely as these, when they weave
Their web among the trinkets of

Formality, at least I forget about love.

South

So I took a walk, the usual remedy, and saw
Monarchs mate on a shoot of melon, overripe,
The orchid wings out-of-place
Above red clay, and beyond the brook
Where suds flow from the development,
Goats agraze in okra: another crop
Too wizened to gather. Then the lake
With no carp to scissor the surface,
More sepia than amber and calm enough

To frame the power plant. On the way back,
However, the sun exposed that image and set
A beer keg—sunken booty—glowing
From the debris. The goats, I assume,
Moseyed to the last clumps of milkweed
By the interstate, where monarchs were
Long gone in a pattern toward Texas.
But that was all right. For a little while
I had shut her out of my mind as a man

Shuts out too many seasons. He yields
To the still life, pasture or postcard,
But not this: a robin too weak to fly
From the path or too sage to follow
The standard migration. I'll never know
Why it picked my place to loiter, the head
Jarred to one side in judgment. I suppose
I should endow a bird with wisdom. I have
Nothing better to do, standing here
Dumb with song, unable to enter an empty house.

Man in the Kitchen

He sits at the table. Sulks. Stares at the wall,
Waiting for the phone there to jingle
More than ring. His daughter settles finally
On the sofa for a nap. He has made the bed,
Mowed the lawn—shopped, shined—

You name it. The woman he loves has her own
Hard life. She could write a book
Or has already. Would it surprise you
She is stronger than a man who makes
Beds? He had ten minutes to scribble a note,

Drop it off. Call, the note said.
Get rid of him and call. He wanted to make
His presence felt, a manly thing perhaps
But a sign: he was sure of himself. Last night
The moon rose full with a yellow haze

Like a ring around it, another sign:
Rain that fails to arrive. The Saturday sun
Shines on his half-open shirt. He toys
With a button, then slides the hand under
To caress a mat of hair on his chest,

Graying. Once all that mattered was her
Nuzzling there, hearing the heart
Thunder in the throes of a passion
Too powerful to allow. A man could
Wallow in it. But this one made a vow

To wait, as he was waiting now,
As one waits for a thundercloud to move
When it seems to hover too long
Over your house. Over mine. The house here
Stays quiet in the early afternoon,

The dog asleep on the patio, the cottonwood
Fluffing the yard with a summery snow,
The freezer not even ahum. Somehow
Desire moves along as a cloud might
And a blue like sky takes its place,

Endless as sky, high as it, but blue
All the same. You have to talk
Your way out of it, long lovely
Talks that go on and on, as the man wanted to,
As every man does. This one hung up,

Gently let her go. This morning he wanted her
Back as a child wants, as his daughter
Wants everything she sees and cannot have.
The man considers this. The call arrives
Sudden as rain, the house alive again

As if shaken by rain. The loneliness
Rises anew. *This is the life
We have chosen*, she whispers. The wall
Closes in on him, and he makes her
Say it again: *this is the life.*

Asylum, at Least on Paper

She takes pen to a poem and sparks it
With metaphor. She writes about love with a hand
Adept at many arts. When she paints, she puts
Our world on canvas, the paper of poverty.
She has knack and skill, but no permit

Society will license or allow. I have
A file-full—degrees, honorary and earned,
And a legal decree for love—but not with her.
We are trying to work this out. We are trying
To slip through checkpoints with no papers:

Tonight the guards are asleep, the borders clear.
Take my hand. So many have fallen before us.

What the Waitress Sees

Her life is like ours. One day
Something went *snap!*, and she found herself
In the service of businessmen. More bread,
They call to her, and she responds

As if known by that name. More Bread.
We want burgundy, lots of it, and then
We would like her to leave. She sees
Couples all the time: married, pretending

To be, not to be, about to be. Yet
We are different. A man of dangerous
Middle Age: suited, tied. And you are younger
Of course: casual, cute. That says plenty,

But how we carry on! How we huddle
Over paper! You yell, redden, are ready
To wash my face with wine. I cannot argue
With you anymore. I reach for a napkin,

A pen. "Don't give me a line," I write,
"Give me a stanza." You are quiet again
So I add, "It will work. Trust me."
In an hour, you tell me *We can't go on*

Like this, I want to be whole for you.
She cannot hear us. But she sees you
Crying now, and no one has raised
A voice. A glass. Or a fist. Later

She finds the napkin with a tip. Stanza?
A type of dance maybe, a Latin one like tango.
Last Stanza in Paris. How we belong there!
But this is Oklahoma, where something goes

Snap! Dancers. She wants us to be dancers
Who stanza in a honky-tonk. She looks
At the clock. She will meet someone tonight.
It will work this time. It will be good.

Liebe und Literatur

The old poets were wrong about travel and love:
How glib it seems now for a man to say to his son
To thine own self be true, and this from one
Whose daughter never made it beyond the orchard; take Jonson
Then, and all those carpe diems to Celia in lieu of
One good kiss, which he didn't get; or Lovelace
Wanting to fly to Althea from prison,
Who of course was at home, not in route anyplace;
They wrote what they wanted to believe, they never could face
A woman true to herself away, and her passion.

Take us, for instance: just when we came so near
To learning whether our love was free will or fate,
You get a job in Germany and I, the old fear
That you will forget, being true to yourself; I will wait
For your letters as Jonson for a kiss, which by the way
You owe me; and I will want to fly to you from the clay
Prison of Oklahoma, thinking you're in route; already it is clear
I cannot write the line I need to believe:
But we will know—carpe diem, be damned!—if you must leave.

The Brevity and Permanence of Snow

All night, as I lay in the spare room
Thinking of us, the snow has been falling
On the car, on the evergreen and hedge. It grows
Sudden and cold as our love. We should revel tonight
In sub-zero, cover the tracks: our souls are together,
Twined as any limb. I can't even wake you.
In the blue-grey light the window allows, you'd see me
Stroking a lock of hair from the delicate cheekbone
I might kiss, and ask me *What are you doing? Why*
Are you awake? You would brush my hand like snow.
I want to whisper, we are alive. We feel the same
Love for the other. But you sleep and I watch
The flurry outside conceal what remains
Of metal and wood. By morning, the snow
May drift like a dream and embed us
Or may melt like beauty and be gone.

Self-Portrait

The night you drew with precision
And purpose, I dreamed of you—or someone
That could have been you—above me, moving.
You were at the loft with a man. I couldn't tell
What world I was in, what bed, and why

In sleep I felt your hair, your breath.
You left to come for me, your mentor.
I took the key and didn't know what
Or whom to expect. And so I saw her,
The woman on canvas, the body

Lithe and clothed, understated,
A face too sure for self-portrait,
A pose too pronounced. The eyes,
Not the hands, held me. The smile,
Not its promise of easy love, lured me:

"Think perspective, think critique,
Talk line and movement—art as object—
Not objective." That was the goal.
But the woman worried me, for canvas
Can be a script of change to come,

Or a creed we adopt out of duty.
I looked at the woman, and she at me.
I considered all angles. Then I remembered
The dreamlike figure above me and knew
As never before: *we had a future*.

Dolphins

All day as we wander again
Miles apart, I take in show after show
At the aquarium. The dolphins
Begin to notice me, deadpan
By the holding tank, their lingo

Primal as love. Like us,
They long to communicate
The next move. They spout off
The top of their heads, literally,
And people laugh at them, underplay

Their genius. Even their genre:
Mammal or fish? They have two names
As we have two names. "Dolphin"
Is pretty enough, but "porpoise"
Sounds too much like another word,

Purpose. What is the purpose
Of a dolphin who leaps 18 feet for a fish?
Another can walk on water. To tell how,
I need the diction of erotica
Or religion. I know the spirit of it

Arises like a god about to jettison
The body. Sleek as it is, an arrow.
I want to be that sharp, that precise.
Lately, though, I see us in everything,
Mammal or fish. Together we are

Buoyant, graceful, agile—adjectival
As poetry when it tries too hard
To say "beauty." But that is your word,
An echo only you can hear
Out of the blue. Louder now than ever.

Angelic Love

> *I invoke you, almost deadly birds of the soul,*
> *knowing what you are*—Rilke

What is it that wants as the body never has, with every corpuscle
Of being, the system immune to shocks of blame and embarrassment,
To all checks and balances that keep custody of the self?

Free from the body you wrap like a wound in my presence,
The terry cloth tight as a tourniquet, your spirit melds
With mine as in afterlife, the glow and glimmer of me

Waiting, years gone, in the tunnel of your last earthly
Illusion. *Don't you know what's happened?* Obsessed with beauty,
Consumed by it, you are on the threshold of its man-begotten mate:

Pain. You are that close, the hair's breath from pinnacle,
And all your angels thought it impossible in the mortal life!
Sure, they oversee the soul. But they would sell out the body,

That merchant who knows love best—the caliber of each
Magnum-chamber of heart, the ion-count of moonbeam on iris,
The syllabics of a kiss and likelihood of its lasting

A nanosecond longer than lips or lungs can bear—
Or conscience. So lost in love, we let the spirit lie
Where the body might have been, feel it rise above us

Like a cloud on sapphire sky, and damn the beauty it undoes
Knowingly as a man who lifts the last slip of silk
From the woman he will kneel before in this world and worship.

Part Three

Discovery

1024/1986

You talk about the world
Unfolding within you, and all I want
Is to cup your elegant face
And lay my lips on yours
The way the most gentle lovers then
Must have kissed on a knoll

In the Netherlands. We go back as far,
The blue of your eyes, a darker blue,
The brown of my eyes, a lighter brown,
Fuller, specked with yellow
Like a leaf that is falling soon. Yet
They are our eyes. We are young

As our leathery colors, sun-bleached,
Loyal. This is a leave-taking
We remember still. Our new bodies
Have always been these bodies, small
As then, powerful, out of place
As anything old is out of place

In this epoch. You talk about acceptance,
And I feel the fate of those early lovers
Whose lips meet in a perfect, startling
O. Their breath, a shared breath.
Their longing, also shared. They have
Never kissed before. Their hearts are adrum

As the horn-call summons from the tower,
A warning: they are going to lose each other.
This is our first life being etched
In the echo-chamber of time. You talk
About power, and I feel that kiss.
I have found you again. We are gods.

The Unnatural Act of Our Making

To speak of soul on the telephone, no less,
Linking us by angel-hair of fiber, the receiver
Easy in your palm, your voice disembodied:
This is how we live. The body is a prison
With lock and untimely combination,

You and I. We mate without touch and escape
As hellions might, on technicality.
There is no escape. Only terror now
To know that muscle has no say in this,
Or will. We carry on with worry-work

Because we are good at it, fabulously
Endowed with imagination: I will lose you
To a man of definable features, flesh and blood,
And you will lose me—or what you see in me—an aura
Aligned with yours. This is the body at war

With one weapon. None of it can happen in a poem
You are writing for me. We have become
That strange. I told you about the body
Deprived of touch, how the soul without warning
Moves in for the slow-kill. I asked you

What are you doing? Beauty, you said, was all
You could say: *beauty.* I should have known
A woman who wants a loveliness more than her life
Would get it, and then give herself
To another out of need. How can I tell you?

No one but us has a clue. Do not phone
And feel my pain, my anger, my envy,
My unholy godforsaken manhood that I lose
Every day for you, and whisper—Christ,
As consolation—*I love you with all of my soul.*

The Half-Life of Love

How often have you begged me to wait, be patient,
Or give space, as if the man you claim somehow
To love, consumes that feeling in the few hours
We meet each week and weigh—as a miser would—
The ever-wavering soul? I weary of this

When all my angels reach for you and the body
Stays put like a stump in a rick-worn wood.
We feed our fire overlong. The gilt hue
We otherwise know as imagination
Engulfs us, or seems to, and the flame comes

No closer. The miser's love is cold
But glows in his head like a hearth. The two-plate
Scale that mesmerizes him with its teetering
Ticks as a timepiece might, or a heart:
Yes, I want you. I want us to flare again and burn.

Carpe Diem: What To Expect In Paradise

I suppose when we die and shed the body we never shared—
Aside from holocaust that fuses everything, limbs to libido,
Me a good decade before you—we will rise to a station
Of etiquette and position, of which the stepladder spirits
Are particularly fond, coupling—if you can call it that—
Banned by angelic order, lest two cherubs atwine in their mist
Achieve ecstacy of seraphim; no, like dominions who aspire
To thrones, or archangels to powers, we will resist the renegade
Cupid whose arrowhead sizzles with light and follow a flightplan
Laid by principalities whose hymns are a hymen of wings,
Endowing us with fission in a high place: again we obey

The Law.

Realism

We began to lose our love because I wanted yours
Before it changed as a portrait often does
Too long on the easel, the brow too furrowed
When you get to it, the complexion gone sinister:
I needed help. After all, it was my face and you were
Painting the worst side. A poet, I gave you lines

Picasso would have cubed to caricature, the forehead
Sloped and primitive, the nose laden with lies.
El Greco was worse. He saw sadness in my chin and lengthened
The agony. Van Gogh worked the ear, and I was deaf
To starry nights with you. And then I met Renoir,
Faces of the innocent, no flaw too great to blur

For art's sake, truth be damned. "Make me look
Like that," I said, and you stepped back. Tilted your head,
Hmmn-ed. So you went to work, mixed a little white
To lighten brow and chin, loosen the lips, flushed the face
Pink again with love. But you left the ear alone, a mark
I must live with, for even Renoir could not master the fool.

Poets in Love

We could, of course, be terrible
In bed. When opposites attract,
Anything is possible: a debate,
Say, not about bottom or top,
But whose idea was it, after all,
For the image that just happens

To appear, thinly guised, in the other's
Villanelle. Maybe all goes well,
Better than it's been, till a head
Lolls on a breast and hears a beat
Not unlike the rhythm of a poem
In progress. Hell breaks loose.

Copyright is discussed at length,
Orgasmically. Foreplay becomes
Free verse without the net.
Sonnets, long dedicated, are disowned
In a huff. Books get burned
With the fervor of born-agains.

Then one of us is ready to sully
The Dickinson line about good lyric,
How it should blow off the top
Of your head, when the other
Responds: *Oh yeah? From now on,
Climax is a rhetorical term.*

There it is. We could play
Like that. Or someone will realize
How we got here in the first place:
My life and yours, on the page
For everyone to see, suddenly ours,
Not for all time but the moment.

The Clock

In all our musings about time, linear and cyclical,
We never could synchronize the sexual clock
Or remove it from our lives: love wasn't the matter
But an act of love that for one right reason or another
We denied ourselves, because we are good and wary
About these things with others, moral almost;
So when the word kept popping up, "desire," entirely
Within our diction, it was not a question of whether
You wanted me or didn't, merely an unset thing:
An alarm that goes off in a dark place and runs down
Slowly like a bell—no, I take that back—like a *man*.

There. I've said it.

Sonata and Fugue, a Love Poem

You adore music, and I did. I know
A thing so miraculous has a side that betrays
A true believer. It took my soul—
Not a large endowment, I admit,
But the only one I had at seventeen—
And handed it back. So when I hear Bach,
Or Mozart especially whose haunting
Sonatas seem simple, beauty abounds
And abandons me. Our love becomes atonal,
In need of renewal: an electric piano

We carry like pall-bearers to the loft.
You attach the legs, metal pegs,
And my heart begins to hurt. I want to
Touch her again, that loveliness,
But can't even help
Put it aright, quaint as a harpsichord
In a chamber. Yet I stay. I linger enough
To hear you play a fugue that mingles
Melodies like our souls. The right hand
Talks and the left replies

In a different clef. They never touch
But make a whole without accompaniment.
You ask this out of love, another
Harmony. And now I know that is all
You need to prove yourself on a scale
Grander than I can compose, if I can
Compose anything these days. *Music,
What thou doest unto me!* No one but me
Believes in you as much. When I have you,
I don't. When I don't, you come back

Any way you please.

Stormy

Another attack. I am woozy still, afloat
On whatever they put me, pumped into me,
Welling up in the bloodstream
Engulfing my body, engulfing you with my body,
Because I want to take you. You come back

Easier than ever on a horse
Leading another horse with a rope,
An Appaloosa that clomps the cobblestone
Street where you live. You are a girl
Blossoming soon in the saddle. This is before

We fell in love, before you even knew
We would have to someday. I am a man
With hair like a mane, and spotted
Like the mane of your half Palomino,
Yellow and brown. My skin is brown:

I am not of this place
Where skin as pale as yours
Reddens in the Big Sky of Indian summer.
I come from the city, and my cleated shoes
Click when I walk. You stop to ask

If I can ride that Appaloosa
Whose name could pass now for my name:
Stormy. Sure, I say, though the only horse
I have ridden is a Shetland
An Italian named Nick at a carnival

Led around a ring, when I was a boy.
Sure, I say. I can ride. Of course
I put the wrong pointy shoe in the stirrup
As if to saddle myself
Backward, and you know that I lie,

Wary of me as I am of you. You put me on
That horse—this is how I learn
To tell the truth—and it flies,
The human-eye of Appaloosa
Coming up white as it stops and rears,

Ready to hurl me like a rodeo clown
Who has gulped a jigger too much
Moonshine between go-arounds. You pull
Alongside me and somehow calm the horse,
Talk to it, talk to me, try to talk me down

As if I am on a ledge of skyscraper.
And I don't listen. You are only a girl
I should be able to ride anywhere with.
So you back off and Stormy does it again,
Flies the other way—stops, rears—

Who knows how I hang on? You have to
Save me from myself, as you were to save me
Over and over. This is no horse, though
I could be falling from one. *I know
You will not let me.* Pale girl, Big Sky girl,

I have hung on long enough.

Stay

We talk about love and look to the stars, cliche
Spangles of light that promise so much
But warm us so little. Their beauty is beyond
Any pen, beyond metaphor—sequins, let's say,

On a not very well-spun velvet. The sky
Slinks tonight, or appears to slink, above a bay
That is really the Arkansas River, near Tulsa.
I should be with another now, but leave her

For home, an empty turnpike I can park along
And get out to gaze—yes, gaze—at the Milky Way:
Orion, Big Dipper and Little, constellations
You want to re-name, if you're clever enough.

I am not clever. Yet I know the name of a woman
Who lolled on my chest and found the crevice
Between muscle and blade. She nestled there,
Ready. But then the soul rose up like moon

Sudden and full on the horizon, false light
Caressing the body. It was not you, but I
Re-named her and held that aura of wakeful sleep,
Sent her without sex into dream, a rem-cycle

So fine I could feel her lashes down to the follicle
Flutter my skin. Or maybe I imagined it. Maybe
It was your voice in the echo-chamber of my mind:
I rose to tuck her limp, luxurious body, and heard

Stay. What a magnificent word! It leads to beauty
Frail as this night: there one moment, gone at the next
Flash of headlight or strobe of plane, a Boeing
In-bound for Wiley Post, gear lowered and landing

Where Leo should be, in the far quadrant. Like magic
The sky goes black again, and a meteor falls
Somewhere west of here, where I should be:
Beside you. I cannot know that you see

The same shooting star up close, watch it burn
Orange to white, a color you call passion,
And put me in that momentary fire. Later
You will tell me that. You make the decision to stay.

Anthem: Love and the Antipodes

Why, when I imagine the love
America forbids like a visa,
I put us in Moscow, spires and snow

Aglow for some reason in green,
Or the Urals in summer—
The uranium under-carpet of Urals—

Killing us with half-life precision
Of Dakota everclear? Dakota,
Where we met. Dakota, where we lived—

If you could call it that—30 below
The latitude and loneliness of a Siberia
We could conquer with certain expertise,

With the ever-embering hearth
Of a tundra-trained lover: imagine,
For one night imagine the silo

Outside your window that stores
Neither milo nor missile,
But elevator and shaft to the antipodes—

Opposite ends of the earth—
Whose coordinates I cannot plot
With map and moon-crescent ruler,

But in sleep and the harmless typography
Of poem, realms America yet allows:
America, that may not dream anymore, or scan.

I Know

Harder things to do than give your body
Up, the golden rope of hair, the touch
I love and lost. I cannot think of any

Reason to remain the understudy:
Bed's a stage; the role (for me) a cinch.
I know harder acts to do. Give your body

To another, or a few, but not to me.
I leave it willingly. It does not matter much
To lose one type of love. Think of any

Body, yet not mine! Let mine be free
Of taint, entanglement. Of kiss or clutch
Or harder things. I could give your body

Up like lent, a wife, a son I never see,
Who has my body type and blood: O, such
Loss is easy with love. Just think of any

Number of things we leave behind, a family,
A horse, a house, a church, and do not flinch.
So I should know the ways to give your body
Up, my love. *But I cannot think of any.*

Moon, Love: Whereof I Swear Never Again to Write

Worse, Oklahoma moon. Big, luminous,
Pure enough to read poetry by
Shakespeare, the balcony scene,
Our hero ababble with love, high

On star and simile, run out
Of metaphor, light—it would seem—
Of language: false dawn. Full of you
I rise (what else?) from dream

And walk the streets, rehearsing
How half-cocked one wakes
A lover: knock or ring, song or rock
Where beam through window breaks

Or silhouettes, more aptly put,
Another man. Call it luck or lack of,
Madness or moon: tonight
I swallow all the lines about love

Being starlit and lyric, romantic
And rhymed. Who knows what nothing
I would have whispered in your ear,
What cliche, if you were listening?

Who cares? The man will leave and I will
Not. You'll say your *wherefores* soon
Enough. And I shall sing no more of love,
Whose mask is still the moon.

Salzburg

You bring your lovers here
As if for approval, the alpine air
Lucky as fate, wind, whatever

Light can pierce the fog
Of this gothic city. The castle
Lords above anyone dumb enough

To trust it. Mozart looked up and knew
You run away to become somebody. You cannot
Help but remember him, the libretto

That jangles the inner chamber
Of your ear, that reminds you
How love can fail, and did for you,

Fool. But you're back again, wiser
You think, with a woman you want
Like nobody else, whose soul you own

If you own anything in this
Miserable world. Yet you manage
To botch it: she's ready to leave

And there's nothing you can do about it
But go as planned to the opera, go through
The motion of liking, as luck would have it,

Die Zauberfloete, a fairy tale
You miss all your life. The irony
Strikes you: quiet and dark

You are with her in the balcony
And think you are dreaming. She wants you
To translate the lyrics—

Bist du mir nun ganz ergeben?—
And you are happy to put
Your lips to her ears, to whisper—

Will you please be mine forever?—
Over and over as operas do
Till you mean what you say

But don't let on: she has to endure it
As one endures a joke of indecent
Color. You lose yourself in the line,

The syllables loll off your tongue,
The act ends. She turns—
Her face has gone soft again—

And you gather her in your arms, thank
Mozart, the music, the castle that stands
For romance, whatever god you invent.

Part Four

Heresy

Have I spoken of absolute
All-encompassing love as an innocent might,
With abandon? The alley-people
Italians call *popolaccio*
Knew how to annihilate the ideal. Yet they needed
An idol to keep them in the cathedral,
So the master Caravaggio painted them one:
A madonna, plump and pleasing
Even in death—a priceless altarpiece—in every way

Beauty's embodiment. He splayed
A drowned prostitute on linen in his shuttered
Studio and hung a lantern like the moon
Above her head, malleable as clay. Everybody
Loved it. The cardinals could imagine
A visionary miracle—the voluptuous, immaculate womb—
But not the swollen belly of a woman
Who has lain too long in water,
Blue as a bruise and as holy. The master

Saw with his soul, which the cardinals wanted
To save, and learned as we have to learn
About love. We seek it with abandon,
The desire to touch, to take or be taken,
Consume or be consumed. Caravaggio knew
Both faces. But he used a woman
Whose spent, Eve-like body was worshipped
Until the heresy of his act became known,
And the cardinals saw what men see on linen.

The Bittersweet Days

How long can it go like this, everything
So unnatural or supernatural? Either
The love is public, eavesdroppers everywhere
Breathing scandal, or telepathic: visitations
Brutal and obvious as a kiss. A man
Can choke in his sleep. Now that you are

Listening, it said, keep the man out of this.
The woman is wild for you. Pay no heed
To the babble you hear moving down
On her. You live, after all, in a threadbare
Flat with no balcony or escape. Maybe
She is weary and wonders *What next?*

This is the future. I cannot stop
The both of you. But I'm asking a little
Time here, okay? Let it untangle the knot.
You are lovely, though—arms as thick as her
Sparrow legs and around them like two
Sets of lovers. Ah, yes. *I can haunt you.*

We don't expect anybody to believe this.
Especially you, tapping sex on the line.
Think of it this way: a man loves a woman
Enough to allow the soul a chance.
When you last heard of them, they were
Bitter. Sweet. Nothing in between.

The Night That Should Have Been Ours

Time, time. I write a title and it taunts me,
For I had hours to give to you, slow
Luxurious ones. Sweeps of the clock.
I canceled. The mountains knew it,
The town—art colony, of course—

Drew curtains, shuttered the shops.
Another time, I told the clerk
Who chose our suite with fireplace,
Top floor with a view I saw you against,
Work of art. You know that fantasy:

I come to you, loved already, and watch
You paint, a private act. How
Positively middle class! And unmanly.
So I understood: bad timing, New Year's Eve
To juggle, two men to answer to:

Resolutions. Soon, you said, two months
And we'll begin again. You stroked
My face, those delicate hands, a healing.
Mountains can wait, you said. It'll be spring,
The snow will melt, and we will keep

Plenty of wood for a fire.

Harmony

She is at the opera as I write, the other man
Beside her perhaps, or will meet her later
For a drink. The usual. The tryst at her place,
How beauty always comes to that, how she plays him
Solo-like, detached in what should be duet.

The memory of Mozart is gone, maybe a note
Remains in the night and warbles *a capella*
From her throat. I cannot imagine a lovelier
Music. And knowing the man who hears it,
Who has—as she puts it—no soul, I hate

How love overlooks a patron and picks,
As it did for Amadeus, the spiritually
Tone-deaf. *Still, he composed. He had to*
Bear the pain as long as the will allowed.
So I console myself, knowing she cannot

Let it go on much longer: soprano without tenor,
Body without beauty, sex without soul.

Art By Association

I could send you letters, passionate
As a poet you might revel in, but reduce
To an anatomic part. Painters do that
Easily as poets leave their symbols,
A rose or vase for one, token homage.

I could start a war. I saw you, an artist,
While others saw the symbol: wife
Or outlet for unrequited love. Another blonde.
They'll read this and outdo me, their lines
Full of prowess. Ego. They'll make you

Goddess, or worse, associate you with one.
By nature, I'll step aside. I'll send you books,
Not—for the love of Christ, literature—
But art: Picasso, Van Gogh, Renoir, Manet,
Men who move you as no poet can. Even me.

Silence

When music went out of my life
Like a woman who leaves no note,
I did not think of you. I pawned
The mandolin. Rosewood and spruce,
The tone—like love—was to sweeten

With time. It or I couldn't wait.
This is a problem. The night before,
You sang a gentle music. The melody,
Of course, was time. But we drank to it.
We curled our arms like clefs and drank

All night. This is another problem,
For when you finally stopped
To see me, your friend in tow—
Christ, of all things, with albums—
I was still at it, soused,

A little cash in my pocket.
I don't remember what was said.
Maybe nothing was said,
Or if it was, nobody heard.
You were gone, and I was left

To the fear of every performer:
Silence. Come back to me now
Like a tune I take by request
And can play, if someone out there
Only will sing a few bars.

The Restoration

I forget how he struck it, with hammer or pick, and don't care
To look it up: *Facts on File*, 1972. I will not name him—
Vandal, villain, thief—nor give the man a pulse, a part
In the schemata. A mother, daughter, wife. He chiseled
The holy heart, the Pieta, and I want him dead as stone.

Like you, she's weaker at the seam. Restored but under watch.
For I know men who cannot bear the beauty, who see it and feel
Hate, antonym of anatomy. They hack at right angles,
Marble or flesh. They come for you when you least expect it—
Sculpt their scars, pierce the body, leave the rest to me.

Sudden Love

For no good reason, we found ourselves
In bed, the getting-there hardly
Original: I carried you
Curled in my arms, near sleep
It seems to me now in mid-life
Haze, lulled by something monstrous
While we moved without mind
On pleasure or pinnacle. Sure,
There was afterglow, the ember
Affection ignites when you wake
Welded to somebody whose future
You share, and can never share,
Though one of us wanted that:

I wanted that. I was the one
Ready too soon, who knew you before
The other I would come
Mercilessly to love. Every minute
She matters. But you mattered
From the start—bells even
When we met close to campus—
The campanile chiming the hour,
Or tolling it, a man come miles
To entangle family and fate,
To separate sisterly soulmates
And marry one who has what we never had:
Time. Without warning, love left us

Wounded somehow, hurt beyond knowing,
A decade of guilt and accusation—
Christ, a decade to kill what began
Easy as muscle and breath. Nothing changes
The heart like hate, and we needed hate
The way lovers need air in their throes.
And then it ended. The fire was out
That sudden. So we pick up
The phone now and can say "love"
Without meaning it. Maybe we smile
When we mimic the word. We hang up,
Go back to the kitchen or TV,
And forget that monster who came

One night and took us by the jugular.

Forgiveness

The woman who loves me
Lets me have it
Whenever I ask, but last night
Between bites of a boiled lobster,
She said *Honey, you don't know
The half of that word.* She shut up
And swallowed. Then she shoved me
This book. So I did some speed reading
While she forked another morsel and lo,

She was right: three meanings,
The first of which I was getting
Regularly. Ask, receive. Ask
And get again. (A cinch
If two or in love.) Next,
The social type. Ask and get
So the two don't slay each other
Tomorrow in the hall. The last really
Rattled my cage—the Christian kind—

The forgive-my-sin-so-I-can-get-ahead
Variety. The money-in-the-bank,
Peter-at-the-gate meaning. She smiled,
Sipped a little burgundy. *What will it
Be tonight, bub?* she inquired. A gate
Opened in the vestibule of my brain
And truth like a turtle dove
Took flight. That woman had me
Cold! I kept reading her book—what else

Could she have on me?—the Greeks
Who knew one hell of a lot
More than we do about this
Never forgave in this fashion. Back then,
You got on your knees and slunk away happy
Zeus didn't unravel the digestive track.
She seemed to know this. I didn't ask
When she picked it up. She had this fork,
See. You wouldn't want to fool with her.

Navigating the Asteroid Belt, Zero Visibility

Oh, no. Here they come again,
Long sinewy clouds on either side
Of the mountain. They could be arms
About to clasp the Piper
Whose pilot has just realized
The poetry of throttle and transponder.
I met a woman. She saw the book

You gave me by Antoine de Saint Exupery
And figured I had a flightplan.
Her eyes were blue as yours
And the pupils like hangars opened
To take me in. Yes, I said,
I can fly with the best of them
On my back. One could describe

My position now as eleven o'clock
And contemplate the coordinates.
One could call this embankment
With an unbelievable slope
The rack of a heretic two cranks
Shy of sainthood. Take your pick,
I can hear you saying:

This world or that. I am going
To remain here and compose
An apology in the rain. I hope
The Piper got home all right
And the heretic went to heaven.
I hope these arms enfolding
The mountain have a little pity.

Blackout, Again, in New York

We could shine like stars in the Soho nebulae,
But without you, the sky has fallen. No Dipper,
No Mars. Only a sliver of moonsmear to remind me
You remain in Oklahoma. Lights everywhere, it seems—
Walk light, stop light, subway, cop and Broadway light,
Amber light of windowpanes that cobblestone the skyline,
Cab light, honk-at-the-light, ambulance and arson light—

But above the East River, another blackout, only a nova-like
Pulse of a Boeing. It becomes the north star, and I follow
White and scarlet loops of light that dot the Triborough
Bridge: toll light, barge light, tugs and Roman candlelight,
Landing gear and runway light, searchlight at LaGuardia.
I am no longer afraid. Book the next flight out.
Only you can lift the canopy and replenish the sky.

How to End a Romance

Snow has a way of falling
Gently when the woman makes up
Her mind, and it was doing that,
Dusting her hair as he hoped
To see it in the later years:
Silvery. They were sitting
By a salt river, having a say
About love. He leaned toward her,
But she shifted on the bench,

Lit a smoke. As I said, snow
Was falling, and now smoke
Rose between them. Don't forget
Breath. Breath is important
In a romance. They could barely see
Each other: snow, smoke, breath.
And the man wore glasses, to make
Matters worse. They were fogging up
In the cold, and his face was raw.

So much for mood. Little waves
Below them would ripple and gnaw
At the snowbank, splash another
Hole in it. Something like salt
Gnawed at his insides, but the woman
Had a word for it: leave. *I am going
To leave you*, she said. Lovers
Say such things. They watch a word
Cut to the heart and then they know

The truth. They go on. Or don't:
They want to be sure. So the woman
Said the word again, and it cut
Deeper to the soul, which also has
A gentle way of falling, to make
Someone old. She got up—
A bad sign at this point—
And took a breath that usually means
The last say in a love affair:

The man prepared himself. You could
See him slogging alone in the snow.
This is how love ends, he thought.
But it was only a rush of air
That a woman beside a river
Allowed herself between puffs
Of a cigarette. Snow, smoke,
Breath. It was important,
All right. It was the beginning.